MY SPECIAL FRIEND
Creating a safe and beautiful world

MY SPECIAL FRIEND
Creating a safe and beautiful world

Toyin Adewumi

Copyright © 2023 by Toyin Adewumi

All rights reserved. No part of this book may be reproduced or used in any manner without written permission of the copyright owner except for the use of quotations in a book review.
For more information, contact: t_adewumi@yahoo.com

First paperback edition 2023

Book design by PublishingPush
Illustrations by Moinak Chakraborty

978-1-80541-177-2 (Hardback)
978-1-80227-942-9 (Paperback)
978-1-80227-943-6 (eBook)

To Naomi,

Thank you for helping us experience joy in its purest form and teaching us patience, perseverance and never to give up.

Thank you for helping us appreciate nature and showing us it's ok to stop to smell flowers and enjoy the magical moments of blowing a dandelion.

To every child, thank you for making the world beautiful.

Hi, my name is Chloe,
and I'm glad you are here.

Come along, and let me tell
you about my friend Naomi.

My friend, Naomi, is very beautiful and never scared to be different. She is very special, just like you and I, but what makes her unique is that she is living with autism.

Autism is a brain disorder that makes the brain function differently.

Naomi is fun to be with, and she likes to make friends. Sometimes she may be overwhelmed, and sometimes she likes to play with people, especially if they engage in activities that are of interest to her.

Although my friend Naomi communicates and socialises with people, this may be in a different style from what you know. But that's ok; after all, everyone is different, so relax and let me tell you more.

Naomi loves to sing and dance.

She is very good with numbers.

She enjoys working on puzzles, and it is amazing how her super ability to focus helps her complete puzzles perfectly and very fast.

Wow!!! You should see how Naomi puts jigsaw puzzles together with confidence and without even looking at the reference picture.

Naomi loves to line up her toys in her chosen order and may get upset if you move them around. She is happy for me to play with her toys, provided that it is not the same toy she has arranged in a particular order.

Naomi loves to play the piano, and she is very consistent and diligent when practising new songs. She is able to compose songs that are pleasant to the ear, melodious and make musical sense. She can play any tune she knows in different keys, even without being taught. I have learnt to play some songs from my friend Naomi.

Naomi has a special ability to recall. Sometimes, she may echo the rules of the game we played in the past over and over again or a television advert she watched some days ago. That's ok; she is learning to string words together.

My special friend Naomi has great listening ears and can hear tiny sounds, like clicks, or loud sounds, like clangs, that we mostly ignore!! Although she does not enjoy loud noises and uses her ear defenders to cope, she appreciates calming sounds. The sound of birds is like beautiful music to her ears, and she enjoys the rustling sound of leaves on a tree.

Naomi has a super brain that sends a lot of signals at the same time, especially when there are many things to see or hear.

When too many signals become overwhelming, she responds to them by covering both ears or even making a loud noise. When you see her do this, please don't stare rudely or laugh at her. You may ask her if she is ok.

I love going to the park with Naomi. We both love to swing, and sometimes we love to go on the slide. We enjoy the merry-go-round too. Weee!!!!!!!!! Round and round we go on the merry-go-round.

Naomi enjoys repetitive behaviour like spinning around, flapping her hands and bouncing; sometimes, she also loves to jump high up.

Her difference tries to set her apart and makes it difficult for her to play with others, but she never gives up.

When naughty children try to be mean to her and tell her she does not belong here, I say, "Stop!!!!!!!!!"

It is good to be kind to others even when they are different from you because no two people are the same. Most of the time, the mean children later become good, and we gain new friends to play and laugh with. Our differences always brought lots of beauty to each game we played, and we enjoyed every single moment we spent together.

Naomi is different, but we are all not the same; our differences make each and every one of us unique.

There are many people in the world living with autism, just like my special friend Naomi. Although they live with autism, they are all very different from each other, just like we are.

We need to be kind to one another, even when we feel that others are different from us.

We should always treat others with respect and kindness, just like we would like to be treated.

Kindness makes the world a happier place for us all. It helps us show our differences without fear and a beautiful world of acceptance as a safe place to grow.

I have now told you a lot about my special friend Naomi. Would you like to tell me about your special friend, please?

Facts

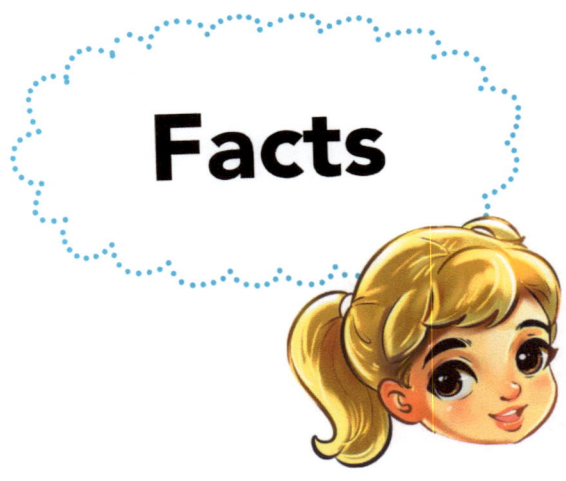

- Autism is a brain disorder that makes your brain function differently.
- When the brain sends too many signals, processing the environment can become very difficult. This can also be called sensory overload.
- Some children living with autism may have trouble communicating, some may have limited words, some are non-verbal and sometimes need some extra support.
- Some children living with autism may find it difficult to cope with loud noises. Ear defenders can help reduce the level of sound.
- Children living with autism like to have new friends too.
- Change can be very stressful for children living with autism. Putting routines in place can help them cope better.
- Children living with autism may need more time to process information and their environment.
- Some children living with autism are sensitive to smell, light, touch, sound and taste.
- Children living with autism may find public places like shopping centres, airports or cinemas very overwhelming. We can make things easier for them by putting support in place and making our environment autistic-friendly.
- Children living with autism may avoid direct eye contact as it can be uncomfortable for them.
- Many adults are also living with autism. This is because autistic children grow into autistic adults.

To learn more about autism,

please visit the National Autistic Society website:

https://www.autism.org.uk/advice-and-guidance/what-is-autism

www.ingramcontent.com/pod-product-compliance
Lightning Source LLC
Chambersburg PA
CBHW042250100526
44587CB00002B/84